T0128418

Other Books by Vinnie Venturella

Sophia's Adventure

I Didn't Write the Memo, I Just Read It.
Selected Poems, Musings
and Leadership Observations

True Leadership: Leadership Lessons
Inspired by the Apostle Paul

Character, Competence, and Commitment…
the Measure of a Leader

Heartbreak Ridge

MEAGHAN'S
LITTLE BOOK OF
WISDOM

VINNIE VENTURELLA

authorHOUSE®

AuthorHouse™
1663 Liberty Drive
Bloomington, IN 47403
www.authorhouse.com
Phone: 1 (800) 839-8640

Published by AuthorHouse 06/05/2019

ISBN: 978-1-7283-1471-6 (sc)
ISBN: 978-1-7283-1470-9 (e)

Print information available on the last page.

This book is printed on acid-free paper.

DEDICATION

This book is dedicated to my oldest daughter Meaghan. She is the apple of my eye and after my own heart. My hope is she achieves her full potential in all things; continues to walk with Jesus Christ; and is a positive example for all she comes in contact with.

INTRODUCTION

June 2019

Have you ever asked, "I wish I knew then what I know now?" Sure, you have, we all have. On the eve of my oldest daughter's graduation from high school, I wanted to provide her that knowledge that she may not have to learn the hard way. We all learn lessons the hard way, but wouldn't you rather not have to?

Even though I've touted these things her whole life and much of my life, never have they all been in one place. I admit I stand for every single one of these and believe wholeheartedly in every single one of these but admit I don't always do these all the time. It's not that I'm hypocritical, it's that I am human and need to try harder.

My prayer is my oldest daughter continues to put these foundational nuggets of wisdom into practice, learns what works for her, and adds more to her list.

Keep our Lord and Savior Jesus Christ first!

Always be yourself.

Say Please and Thank
you early and often.

Treat everyone as you
want to be treated.

Save 10 – 20% of your money your entire working life.

Read every day.

Find God's purpose for your life and fulfill your purpose your whole life.

Conduct physical exercise
every day of your life.

Spend less than you make.

Be a Lifetime Learner.

Eat sensibly every day.

Maintain a healthy weight.

Losing weight is pretty simple, but a lot of people want to over-complicate it. Burn more calories than you take in and you'll lose weight.

The two most effective ways to lose or maintain your weight are eating sensibly or conducting physical exercise or both.

You are beautiful just the way you are. Don't fall for someone else's expectations of you.

Respect your Mom
and Dad.

Be a great example
at all times.

No whining, no
complaining, and make
no excuses – ever.

You are responsible
for your actions.

Consider a daily regimen of stretching and/or yoga your entire life. Flexibility is a magic elixir for the body.

Always, always, always
be the big sister Sophia
wants and needs.

Always do the right thing.

You're never wrong
doing what's right.

Always wear your seatbelt.

Stay 100% focused
on driving, when
you're driving.

Make daily Bible readings
a lifelong habit.

Attempt to get up from bed and go to bed at the same times every day. Staying on a schedule makes you more productive.

Have an attitude
of gratitude.

Your Attitude, not your
Aptitude, will determine
your Altitude.

Self-talk is hugely powerful.
Positive things generate
positive things. The reverse
is also true. Always make
your self-talk positive.

Whether you think
you can or think you
can't – you're right.

You are not a victim. Never, never, never play the victim card.

When necessary say "yes" when the whole world is saying "no."

When necessary say
"no" when the whole
world is saying "yes."

Smile.

Remember everyone
you meet is dealing
with something hard
that you do not see.

Encourage others.

Publicly profess your Faith.

Help those less fortunate
than yourself.

If it was easy, anyone could do it. Things that are worthy are sometimes difficult.

Sometimes it's not the destination but the journey that is most important.

Do not tolerate bullying.

Always remember
your Mom's birthday
and Mother's Day.

When someone in a customer service role does a good job, tell them. Too many times, people only bring up the negative.

Your character is built during adversity. It is also revealed during adversity.

Integrity is doing
what is right when
no one is looking.

Your reputation will precede
you. Make it great.

Be able to be counted on, no matter when, no matter where, no matter why, no matter what.

Always, always, always
do what you say
you're going to do.

If you have to work that
day, go to work and work.

Positive Attitude has healed more illness and sickness than any other remedy on this planet.

Always iron your clothes.

Always be on time.

Sometimes you should
be early to things.

Never be late to
anything, ever.

Leaders lead.

Be a great follower
at all times.

Be a great leader when
that is what is required.

Multitasking is oftentimes a myth. You can only do one thing really well at a time.

Exceeding the standard
should be your standard.

We are what we
repeatedly do.

Competition is good
at times – always be
a good winner.

Stay ready and you'll
never have to get ready.

Stay in shape and you'll
never have to get in shape.

Stay hydrated and you'll
never have to get hydrated.

Talk with your
Mom every day.

Tell your Mom that you
love her every day.

Pray every day.

Simplify your life along the way. Too many people have too many things going on that are time, energy, money, or relationship wasters.

Remember the reason
for the season.

Never sacrifice your
core values for anyone
or anything.

Be kind to people.

Be kind to animals.

Give your money to
worthy causes.

If you budget your
money your entire life,
you'll be amazed at what
you can truly afford.

Don't waste things.

Be thankful.

Cherish those special
moments.

True friends will always
be there when needed.
That's what makes
them true friends.

Always be there for
your true friends.

Be respectful to people.

Do not consort with
bad people.

Weight lifting has been proven to be great exercise for many reasons. Don't fall for the myth of being a female and weight lifting.

Remember, getting
something on sale is not
worth it if you never
needed it to begin with.

Having a relationship with Jesus means you can talk with Him about anything, anywhere, anytime.

Never let a man
hit you – ever.

People deserve second chances, until they don't.

Floss and brush your
teeth at least once daily.

Learn how to type.

Never use tobacco or
tobacco substitutes.

Drink in moderation.

Always tell the truth.

Be consistent.

Support those above you.

Support those below you.

If you don't stand
for something, you'll
fall for anything.

Be special every day
and you will never
regret your life.

Never let a man
disrespect you.

If you know you're
right, who cares what
others think?

Be great at your job.

Never slack off.

You are being paid to do
a job – do your job.

Find out what you're
truly passionate about
and do that.

Achieve your potential.

Fulfill your destiny.

Understand current events but don't let them get you down.

Do not litter.

Maximize your employer's
retirement plan.

Invest your entire
working life.

Educate yourself about
personal finance.

Things are never as bad
as they first appear.

Worrying about things is a waste of time and energy.

Decisions aren't as hard as people will make you think they are, as long as you follow your values.

Be decisive.

Don't be wishy washy.
Make a decision and
move forward.

Just because it's simple
doesn't mean it's wrong.
A lot of times the simple
answer is the best answer.

Don't over complicate things.

Know the difference
between right and
wrong and always do
the right thing.

If given a choice,
compliment instead
of criticize.

It's not fair, but people make judgements about you and your family by how you look in public.

You need less sleep than
you think you do.

Make sure to get
adequate sleep.

Never quit.

Nothing great is accomplished without some difficulty. Greatness forges through adversity.

Be a person of character.

People are known by a lot
of things. Being known
as a person of character is
about as good as it gets.

Always smile and greet
people that you pass by.

Be the light in
someone's day.

If you quit, you'll be a
quitter your whole life.

Most television and
social media are garbage.
Use in moderation.

Everything you put
online is permanent.

At your current employer, remember you are on a job interview every day.

Sophia has looked up to you her whole life and will continue to do so. Be the example worthy of being looked up to.

There is a debate in society on the value of educational degrees. Strive to become as educated as possible.

John Wayne said
"Life is tough but it's
tougher if you're stupid."
Think about that.

Don't waste time.

Illogical people don't know
they're being illogical.

Trying to use logic with an illogical person is wasted time and energy. Move on.

Good or bad, what comes
out of your mouth, is from
your heart. Strive for good.

Strive to generate as many income streams as you can, especially in retirement.

The only place success
comes before work is
in the dictionary.

Don't spend one dollar
on a ten-cent decision.

Haters will always hate.

Know that it doesn't matter what you do, you will never please everyone, so don't try.

Vote during elections.

Life isn't fair – still
do the right thing.

Beware of people who are always trying to get over on other people, over on the man, or over on the system.

Everyone that you meet
knows something you
don't, learn from them.

Shady kids and shady young people grow up to be shady adults.

If someone is going to be
dishonest in little things
they're probably going to
be dishonest in big things.

The harder you work
the luckier you'll get.

If you lose at something,
don't lose the lesson.

Come on, come on,
let's go, let's go.

When dealing with life's
issues keep the big picture
uppermost in mind.

Just because people disagree with you doesn't mean you're wrong.

Just because you think you're right, doesn't mean you are.

Stand at attention and place your hand over your heart whenever the National Anthem plays.

Remember your Mom
has way more experience
than you do being a
woman; heed her advice.

Park your vehicle so you can always pull out…always.

Learn how to cook and
make your own meals
as much as you can.

Never underestimate the huge positive impact you can have on people around you. Don't waste the opportunity.

Contribute the maximum
amount you're allowed
to in a Traditional IRA
or Roth IRA, every year
of your working life.

Good or bad – choices
have consequences –
good or bad.

No one owes you anything.

Take what you do
seriously, but don't take
yourself too seriously.

Protect your personal
data at all costs.

Be open to feedback.

The best and most effective way to avoid hospitals, doctors, and healthcare expenses is to be as healthy as possible. Prevention is critical.

Aside from a mortgage
that you can easily
afford, you should never
have any debt – ever.

Have as much life insurance as appropriate for every member of your family.

Decide to be better
not bitter.

Be loyal to your faith, family, then nation, in that order, and then everything else after those three.

Always keep your
things, and your house
neat and orderly.

Pay attention to detail.

Always be aware of
your surroundings.

Good things don't normally
happen after midnight.

Think twice before
you push "send."

Talking smack on text, email, internet, social media – wherever, can never be taken back.

Sticks and stones may break bones, but words hurt more than you think.

It takes courage to lead. Most people won't step out front. A lot of them will ridicule you if you fail. Have the courage to lead anyway.

If your meal and service were good, or especially if they were exceptional, tip well.

You get what you pay for.

Being thrifty with
your money is prudent;
but don't be cheap.

Eat what you are
given when you are at
someone else's house.

Never go to a special event at someone's house empty handed. Flowers, wine, or a book are always appreciated by the host.

You normally can never over-dress for an event, but you can sure under-dress for an event.

Always pay your
bills on time.

If something doesn't
feel right or seem right,
you're probably right.

Always give yourself plenty of time to brake, regardless of road, traffic, or weather conditions.

Maximize the gifts
God has given you.

Every failure is
an opportunity to
learn and grow.

Admit when you're wrong
and move forward.

Be the first to volunteer.

You will have vastly more success than most people in everything and anything, simply by showing up prepared.

Be humble.

Actions speak louder
than words.

Your silence during critical times will be deafening.

Say what you mean and
mean what you say.

Forgiveness is as much
for you as it is for the
one being forgiven.

Listen more and talk less.

Most people want to be and try to be good people. Assume the best of intentions.

Instead of asking God
for stuff, thank Him
for all His blessings.

There is as much physiological, spiritual, psychological, and mental benefits in exercise as there are physical benefits.

Don't be reckless but
take risks from time to
time. The fruit is at the
end of the branches.

Stock markets move up and down over short periods of time, but they always go up over the long term. Use this to your advantage.

The world needs leaders.
The world especially needs
strong female leaders.
Continue to be that
strong female leader.

Printed in the United States
By Bookmasters